King Lear
Classroom Questions

A SCENE BY SCENE TEACHING GUIDE

Amy Farrell

SCENE BY SCENE
ENNISKERRY, IRELAND

Scene by Scene
11 Millfield, Enniskerry
Wicklow, Ireland.
www.scenebysceneguides.com

King Lear Classroom Questions by Amy Farrell. —1st ed.
ISBN 978-1-910949-35-1

Contents

Act One, Scene One

Points to Consider

The main focus of this scene is Lear's division of his kingdom, and the love test he sets his daughters.

Some students will find fault straight away with Lear for demanding this profession of love from his daughters, and will sympathise with Cordelia who does not flatter her father. Lear's harsh treatment and disowning of his youngest daughter will cause many students to form a negative first impression of him, viewing him as a cold, conceited, cruel old man. Some will also feel that this division of his kingdom is in itself a very foolish move, as he is effectively stripping himself of power and throwing himself at the mercy of his eldest children.

Lear's treatment of Kent, who tries to reason with him, may compound students' first impressions of Lear as someone stubborn and unwilling to listen to reason.

Students tend to admire France for his treatment of Cordelia and willingness to wed her when Lear has disowned her.

Students may feel sorry for Gloucester's illegitimate son, Edmund, in this scene, based on the way Gloucester refers to the situation surrounding his birth.

Questions

1. How does Gloucester refer to each of his sons?

2. What does Lear plan to do to his kingdom when we first meet him?

3. How does Goneril describe her love for her father?

4. How does Regan describe her love for her father?

5. How does Cordelia describe her love for her father?

6. Why doesn't Cordelia flatter her father as her sisters do?

7. How does Lear treat Cordelia's honesty?

8. What would you do in Cordelia's situation?

9. Why is Kent banished?

10. How does Burgundy react, now that Cordelia has lost her riches?

11. How does France respond?

12. What does Cordelia ask her sisters to do before she leaves?

13. How do her sisters treat her at this time?

14. What do you think of the way Cordelia's family treat her?

Act One, Scene Two

Points to Consider

In this scene Edmund reveals his plan to turn his father against his brother Edgar, and so lay claim to Edgar's rightful inheritance. He is established as a wicked character, while his gullible father believes him all too quickly and is easily deceived.

Students will realise Edmund's villainous traits after seeing how easily he misleads and manipulates his father and brother.

Questions

1. Why does Edmund feel hard done by?

2. What is the significance of the letter Edmund carries with him?

3. How would you describe Edmund, based on what we have seen so far?

Act One, Scene Three

Points to Consider

Some students may be slow to feel that Goneril is treating her father poorly, as his treatment of Cordelia will still be fresh in their minds. It may be necessary to remind them of the pledges of love she made to him, and to point out how she has benefitted significantly from her early inheritance. The idea of filial duty could be introduced and discussed at this point.

Questions

1. How does Goneril treat her father?

2. How does she speak about her father with her servant, Oswald?

3. What does she decide to do about King Lear?

Act One, Scene Four

Points to Consider

Students tend to admire Kent's loyalty here. He refreshes his service to the King, despite the poor treatment he has received from him.

It may be necessary to draw attention to the function of the Fool here, so that students will anticipate his truthful statements and watch out for them.

Although all will agree that Goneril treats her father poorly here, not all may sympathise with his plight. Some may feel that Lear placed himself in a vulnerable position and should have been prepared for this outcome.

Questions

1. Why has Kent returned, even though he is banished?

2. What does Oswald do that angers Lear?

3. Why is the Fool in low spirits when we meet him?

4. The Fool tells Lear, "Thou hadst little wit in thy bald crown, when thou gavest thy golden one away". What does this mean?

5. What does the Fool mean when he says "thou madest thy daughters thy mothers" to Lear?

6. Why does Lear want to have the Fool whipped?

7. What complaints does Goneril make to Lear about his behaviour?

8. What punishment does Lear want Nature to inflict on Goneril for the way she's treated him?

9. What does Lear decide to do next?

10. What kind of person is Lear, based on what we have seen of him so far?

11. Consider Lear's treatment of his daughters and those around him, his opinion of himself and his personality.

Act One, Scene Five

Points to Consider

Once again the Fool tells Lear the harsh truth about the situation he is in, telling him he won't receive any better treatment from Regan than he did from Goneril.

Lear is beginning to suffer emotionally in this scene, exclaiming that he doesn't want to go mad. It is worth pointing this out, as a precursor of what is to come.

Questions

1. The Fool says, "Thou shouldst not have been old till thou hadst been wise."
   What does he mean by this?

2. What is your view of Lear's mental state, at this time?

Act Two, Scene One

Points to Consider

In this scene Edgar becomes the third good character to have exile forced upon him (he joins Cordelia and Kent).

Edmund easily fools both his brother, Edgar and his father, Gloucester, in this scene and seizes the position of Gloucester's rightful heir.

Regan's visit is due to her desire to speak with Goneril, without Lear present.

Questions

1. How does Edmund confuse his brother?

2. How does Edmund explain his injury to Gloucester?

3. Regan says, "What, did my father's godson seek your life?" What is the significance of this statement?

4. What is your opinion of Edmund? Explain your answer.

Act Two, Scene Two

Points to Consider

Kent's behaviour here mirrors that of Lear. He engages in conflict and loses self-control, as Lear has done. The reason for this behaviour is loyalty to his King.

Questions

1. Why is Kent so angry with Oswald?

2. How does Cornwall treat Kent?

3. What is your opinion of Kent at this stage?

Act Two, Scene Three

Points to Consider

In this scene, Edgar transforms himself into the beggar, Poor Tom, the disguise he intends to utilise. His new appearance foreshadows what will become of Lear.

Questions

1.   What does Edgar tell us he intends to do in his soliloquy?

Act Two, Scene Four

Points to Consider

In this scene, Lear's relationship with Goneril and Regan breaks down entirely. They refuse to grant him the number of knights he desires and he feels disrespected and badly treated. Students will enjoy discussing the cruel way that Lear's daughters treat him, and many will sympathise with the King, particularly when they see the strain that he is under.

It is worth noting how the imagery of the raging storm reflects the turmoil in Lear's mind as the scene ends.

Questions

1. What is Lear wondering about when the scene opens?

2. What kind of imagery does the Fool refer to?
   What is the effect of this?

3. What does Lear refuse to believe?
   What makes Lear annoyed with Regan?

4. How does Lear describe Goneril to Regan?

5. How does Regan react to this?

6. How does Regan speak to Lear?

7. Why is Lear convinced that Regan will not mistreat him?
   (line 175 onwards)
   Is he foolish to think like this?

8. How does Lear describe Goneril at this point?

9. How would you describe Lear's emotional state in this
   scene?

10. What is the significance of the storm at the end of this Act?

11. How would you describe the way Lear's daughters are
    treating him at this point? Explain your answer.

Act Three, Scene One

Points to Consider

King Lear is suffering significantly at this point, and the storm imagery lends itself well to this.

A hopeful note is introduced with the mention of Cordelia's return.

Questions

1. How is Lear coping at this point? Describe his behaviour to support your viewpoint.

2. What is the Fool's role?

3. What does Kent reveal to the Gentleman?

Act Three, Scene Two

Points to Consider

Students should be able to assess Lear's current mental state and to explain the reasons why he is thus affected.

Students may also notice a softening in Lear, he now begins to consider others, in this case, the Fool.

The loyalty and devotion of Kent and the Fool are worth noting.

Questions

1. Describe Lear at this point.

2. How does Lear refer to himself in this scene? (line 18-19)

3. Describe the weather conditions in this scene.

4. Lear calls himself "a man more sinn'd against than sinning".
   What does this mean?
   Do you agree with him here?

5. How does Kent support Lear in this scene? Explain your answer.

6. Is there a change in Lear's attitude? Explain.

Act Three, Scene Three

Points to Consider

Gloucester views the treatment of Lear at the hands of his children as 'unnatural'. It can be interesting to hear students' views on this.

Students tend to be shocked by Edmund's deception of his father and wicked intentions here. This makes Edmund's character and motivation interesting to discuss.

Questions

1. What does Gloucester think of the way Goneril and Regan have treated their father?

2. What mistake has Gloucester made in this scene?

3. How would you describe the way Edmund treats his father, Gloucester?

Act Three, Scene Four

Points to Consider

The storm on the heath mirrors the storm that is raging within Lear.

This is the first instance where we see Lear thinking of others, in particular those less fortunate and well off than himself.

Lear's reaction to his daughters' ingratitude and harsh treatment threatens to overwhelm him and drive him mad. Some students will sympathise, others may feel his response is over the top, or out of proportion. It can be interesting to discuss these views, as this will help students to develop their view of Lear himself and his offspring.

There is a focus here on mental suffering and the idea of being driven to madness, which is worth noting.

Gloucester appears favourably in this scene as he helps the harried King, as do Kent and the Fool.

Questions

1. Why does Lear want to endure the storm?

2. How has Lear changed from the King we met in the first Act?

3. Lear asks Poor Tom, "Didst thou give all to thy daughters?"
   What does this tell us?

4. The Fool says, "This cold night will turn us all to fools and madmen."
   How appropriate is this comment?

5. Why does Lear tear off his clothes?

6. Gloucester tells Kent that Lear's "daughters seek his death".
   Are you shocked by this development?

7. Why does Lear consider Poor Tom to be a philosopher?

8. Lear seems to think he and Tom are similar, but which character is really similar to Tom (Edgar)?

Act Three, Scene Five

Points to Consider

Edmund's character is further revealed in this scene, as he betters his own position at his father's expense.

Questions

1.   What has Edmund done to his father?

2.   How does Edmund benefit from this?

Act Three, Scene Six

Points to Consider

Edgar's references to the "foul fiend" add to the dark imagery in this scene.

Lear's madness is evident as he conducts the mock-trial of his wayward daughters, who are not in fact present for the event. The toll their actions have taken on him is shockingly clear.

The Fool's final words are somewhat cryptic here. Is he calling it a day halfway through the play (at noon?), because the King's obvious disintegration is too much for him? Are the tragic consequences that are to follow clear to the Fool? Does he simply have nothing more to contribute?

It can be interesting to discuss the Fool's last words with students, as he disappears completely from the play after this scene. In some performances of *King Lear*, the Fool is hanged; this explains his absence and non-participation after this point. (Lear mentions that, "my poor Fool is hanged" in Act Five, Scene Three, which may explain his hanging here. If so, this foreshadows Cordelia's fate at the play's end.) This can be worth discussing with students from a stagecraft and performance point of view.

Questions

1. What does Kent want Lear to do?

2. What is Lear doing?

3. What does this tell us about his state of mind?

4. The Fool says "And I'll go to bed at noon".
   These are his final words in the play. Why do you think
   Shakespeare does this?

5. What plan does Gloucester have?

6. Edgar says "He childed as I fathered." What does this mean?

7. Does Edgar find it difficult to keep up the constant
   pretence of pretending he's Poor Tom?
   Explain your answer.

8. Are you hopeful for the King in his current position?
   Explain your stance.

Act Three, Scene Seven

Points to Consider

Gloucester's suffering in this scene parallels that of Lear.

This scene exhibits the depths of cruelty that Lear's daughters are capable of. Students may be surprised that female characters are so vicious and brutal, as it is not in keeping with female stereotypes. Shakespeare's portrayal of women here is worth discussing.

The actions of the First Servant on Gloucester's side echo the interventions of Gloucester himself earlier in the play. Just as he helped Lear, now he is being helped. The servant's wounding of Cornwall is the first blow suffered by the wicked characters. Despite the evil evident in this violent scene, there is still evidence of goodness and humanity.

Regan reveals to Gloucester that it was his favoured son who betrayed him, and he instantly regrets his treatment of Edgar.

Questions

1. Regan and Goneril are determined to punish Gloucester for helping Lear. They say "Hang him instantly" and "Pluck out his eyes". What do you think of this?

2. Is it significant that Edmund is not present to see how his father is treated?

3. What reasons does Gloucester give for helping Lear?

4. What do you think of the First Servant's actions?

5. What do you think of Cornwall and Regan's treatment of Gloucester?

6. Gloucester says "All dark and comfortless. Where's my son Edmund?" Comment on the fact that Gloucester looks for Edmund in his hour of need.

7. What is your reaction to Gloucester's blinding?

8. What is important about the servants' reactions in this scene?

9. What does this scene tell us about justice?

10. What does this scene tell us about human nature?

11. Why is this scene a major turning point in the play?

Act Four, Scene One

Points to Consider

It is very difficult for Edgar to witness his father's afflictions in this scene. This suggests a kind and forgiving character.

Gloucester is full of misery and despair, and realises how he has mistreated his son. It can be interesting to discuss his predicament and compare his situation to that of Lear.

Questions

1.   Describe Edgar's mood at the beginning of this scene.

2.   Describe Gloucester's mood as the scene opens.

3.   How has Gloucester's attitude to Edgar changed?

4.   How does Gloucester treat Poor Tom and the Old Man?

5.   What makes this scene sorrowful?

6.   What similarities do you notice between Gloucester and Lear at this stage?

Act Four, Scene Two

Points to Consider

Albany has turned against his wife (Goneril) and is appalled at her unnatural treatment of her father and the savage blinding of Gloucester. His speeches here are full of imagery rich in reference to monsters and wrong-doing.

Meanwhile, Goneril now has designs on Edmund, he has become the object of her affections.

News reaches the castle that Cornwall has died as a result of his wounds, a fact Albany interprets as proof of the justice of Heaven. Goneril focuses not on questions of justice, but on the fact that Regan is now free to marry again. She fears that Regan may form a relationship with Edmund. This emerging love triangle is something that students tend to enjoy discussing, in relation to what it says about the sisters and their relationship with one another.

Questions

1. We hear of a change in Albany's character.
    What is different about him?

2. What developments are there between Goneril and
    Edmund?

3. What does Goneril mean by the following?
    "O the difference of man and man!
    To thee a woman's services are due:
    My fool usurps my bed."

4. Describe Albany and Goneril's relationship at this point.

5. Comment on how Albany and Goneril speak to one
    another and the language they use to describe
    one another.

6. How does Albany react to the news of Cornwall's death?

7. How does Goneril react to the news of Cornwall's death?

8. What are Albany's intentions as the scene ends?

Act Four, Scene Three

Points to Consider

In this scene we learn that France has returned home, so an invasion is now out of the question. It can be interesting to discuss this development; some students will feel that help was never going to arrive, others will still hold out for a happy (or close to happy) ending.

It is worth commenting on Cordelia's reaction when she reads of how her sisters have treated Lear. Some students will view her as a thoroughly 'good' character, others will feel she is too forgiving, considering how cruelly her father treated her.

In connection with the previous point, some students will have little sympathy for Lear, and will feel it is only right that he is ashamed and afraid to face Cordelia. Others will feel he has suffered enough already and is due a loving reconciliation with his youngest daughter.

Questions

1. Where is France as the scene opens?

2. How did Cordelia react when she read about how Lear had been treated by Goneril and Regan?

3. What is Kent's belief regarding how characters and personalities are formed?

4. Why doesn't Lear want to see Cordelia?

5. Comment on the mood and atmosphere at this point.

Act Four, Scene Four

Points to Consider

It is interesting to discuss Cordelia here as she is presented on stage and to consider her motivation for going to war against her home country.

Questions

1. How does Cordelia describe Lear as the scene begins?

2. What does Cordelia promise to anyone that can restore Lear's sanity?

3. Why is Cordelia going to war against Britain, her home nation?

4. Do you think most people would behave as Cordelia does, in her position?

Act Four, Scene Five

Points to Consider

In this scene Regan is very curious and suspicious about the contents of Goneril's letter to Edmund. Her jealousy here can make for lively classroom discussion.

Her words about Gloucester further emphasis her cruel nature.

Questions

1. Why is Regan interested in Goneril's letter?

2. What mistake does Regan think they made with Gloucester?

3. Where does she think Edmund has gone?

4. What suspicions does Regan tell Oswald about?

5. What do you make of Regan's behaviour in this scene, considering her husband has died so recently?

Act Four, Scene Six

Points to Consider

In this climactic scene, the twin fates of Lear and Gloucester are brought together.

Edgar saves his despairing father from suicide by deceiving him. He convinces him that his 'survival' of this attempted suicide is miraculous and that the gods wish him to live. Some students will feel that it was unfair for Edgar to trick his father this way, while others will argue that it was for the best.

Students may also like the fact that Edgar is no longer in disguise as this scene closes, but has now returned to his true self. They may anticipate a show-down with his brother, Edmund.

When Lear appears on stage he is still consumed with how he has been mistreated by his daughters. The dark imagery here is worth noting.

Gloucester is clearly moved when he sees how troubled Lear is and forgets his own problems and situation.

Edgar's defence of his father is worth discussing. Some will feel he has always been a truly devoted son, and his fight with Oswald is part of this. Others may feel that he did too much for his father, considering how his father treated him in return. Edgar's behaviour and that of Cordelia are worth discussing and comparing.

Edmund's intercepted letter provides Edgar with proof of his brother's scheming and wrongdoing.

Questions

1. What change does Gloucester notice in Edgar?

2. What does Gloucester intend to do at the cliff edge?

3. What does Edgar claim happens when Gloucester 'jumps' from the cliff?

4. Why does Edgar mislead his father like this?

5. What is significant about Lear's appearance when he arrives in this scene?

6. How does Gloucester react to the sound of Lear's voice and what does this tell you about Gloucester?

7. Explain Lear's speech beginning at line 105 and comment on what it shows you about his character.

8. How does Edgar react to the sight of Lear? (line 138)

9. What opinion does Lear give about authority and justice? (line 152)

10. Describe Lear's emotional state in this scene.

11. How does Gloucester change in this scene?

12. What is significant about Oswald's part in this scene?

13. What does Goneril's letter to Edmund reveal?

14.   If you were Edgar, would you be so willing to help your
        father, Gloucester, considering how he treated you?

Act Four, Scene Seven

Points to Consider

Cordelia's good and kind traits are clearly seen in this scene. She is noble and true where her sisters are base, cunning and deceitful. She holds nothing against Lear and pities him for the misfortunes he has suffered.

Students generally find the re-union of Lear and Cordelia satisfying as it has been long-anticipated. Few students will argue that Cordelia is too quick to forgive her father; by this stage most accept that his other daughters have tormented him horribly. Also, Cordelia's character is well established as one incapable of such cruelty or harshness as to punish her already depleted father.

Questions

1. How does Cordelia treat Kent?

2. What does Cordelia think of her sisters' treatment of their father?

3. How does Lear react to seeing Cordelia again?

4. Why does Lear tell Cordelia, "If you have poison for me, I will drink it"?
   What is your reponse to this?

5. What impending event increases the tension as this scene ends?

6. Do you think Cordelia is too quick to forgive her father, considering how he treated her in Act One?

7. Describe Cordelia's character.
   What are her main personality traits?

Act Five, Scene One

Points to Consider

Students tend to enjoy the jealousies developing due to Goneril and Regan's love rivalry over Edmund. They also tend to enjoy Edmund's cruel handling of the situation and the fact that he truly loves neither of them.

Edgar's visit to Albany casts him as something of a hero, he is rising to the occasion to do what is right here.

Questions

1. What information is Edmund seeking at the beginning of the scene?

2. What information is Regan seeking?

3. What is Goneril's priority at this stage?

4. How does Albany view the French invasion?

5. What does Edgar reveal to Albany?

6. What is Edmund's attitude to Goneril and Regan?

7. Does he intend to do as Goneril wishes?

8. What fate is Edmund planning for Lear and Cordelia?

9. What do you think will happen to Goneril and Regan?

10. What do you think will happen to Lear and Cordelia?

Act Five, Scene Two

Points to Consider

In this scene the stage directions indicate that Cordelia's army are retreating in defeat. This is something that students may not pick up on straight away if it is not pointed out to them.

Gloucester is despairing, but is encouraged onwards by his faithful son, Edgar. It can be interesting to discuss the relationship between Edgar and his father here, and also the fact that Cordelia's forces are unsuccessful.

Questions

1. What bad news does Edgar deliver to his father?

2. What does Gloucester's line, "No further, Sir; a man may rot even here," tell us about him at this stage?

3. How has Edgar's character developed up to this point?

4. How does this scene add to the story?

Act Five, Scene Three

Points to Consider

Students are often moved by the fact that Lear looks forward to life in prison, for he will have Cordelia with him.

Some students may be infuriated by Edmund's plan to have Lear and Cordelia executed, they will hope for an intervention to prevent this from happening.

Students tend to enjoy the squabbling and rivalry between Goneril and Regan, seeing it as only fitting that this evil pair should hold no true loyalty towards one another. Some may be shocked to learn that Goneril has poisoned her sister, Regan, as she views her as a love rival. Expect comparisons to talk-show programmes and films surrounding this jealousy over Edmund.

Edgar's arrival and battling with Edmund appeals to students' sense of justice. Generally, they are happy to see Edgar triumph over his wicked brother.

Albany does a lot in this scene to uncover truth and restore order. However, the issues between Goneril and Regan and the fight between Edgar and

Edmund cost him vital time when it comes to the possible saving of Lear and Cordelia. Some students will be frustrated by this.

Students may be unsurprised and unmoved by the deaths of Goneril and Regan. It is interesting in classroom discussion to ask what their deaths say, not only about their own characters, but also that of Edmund.
The tension is increased when Edmund has a change of heart and reveals his orders to have Cordelia and Lear killed. Some students may suggest that this says something good about him and shows something redeeming about his character.

Generally, students will be moved by Lear's heart-wrenching grief when he appears on stage with Cordelia's body. However, a small minority may feel that Lear is truly responsible for her death, as he set the events in motion that led up to this moment. Others may argue that because she forgave him, we, as an audience, should too.

Some students may point out that Kent's appearance at the end of this scene prevents it from being thoroughly depressing and gloomy, for he is a loyal and true character, reminding Shakespeare's audience of the goodness of humanity.

Most students will pity Lear as he dies of a broken heart. It can be interesting to discuss the various effects the deaths in this final scene have on us as an audience, from a personal response point of view.

Questions

1. How does Lear view prison life with Cordelia?

2. Describe Lear's emotional state now that he has been reunited with his daughter.

3. Edmund orders the execution of Lear and Cordelia. How does he justify this?

4. How does Albany intend to deal with Britain's enemies?

5. What reason does Edmund give Albany for imprisoning Lear and Cordelia?

6. What causes the disagreement between Goneril and Regan in this scene?

7. What declaration does Regan make to Edmund?

8. Goneril asks, "Mean you to enjoy him?" Explain why this question is both crude and cruel.

9. How does Goneril view her sister's illness?

10. Why does Albany challenge Edmund?

11. Would you describe Edgar as brave or fearful when he challenges his traitorous brother? Explain.

12. How does Goneril react when her affair with Edmund is uncovered?

13. What reason does Edgar give for the gods punishing Gloucester with blindness?

14. What has happened to Gloucester?

15. What has happened to Kent?

16. What did Goneril do because of her love for Edmund?

17. Why does Edmund want to save Lear and Cordelia?

18. What is the effect on the audience of Edmund's last minute attempt to save Lear and Cordelia?

19. How would you describe Lear's condition when he arrives with Cordelia's body in his arms?

20. How do you know he finds her death difficult to accept?

21. How do the audience feel as the final curtain closes? Explain.

22. Is this a satisfying ending? Explain your view.

23. What does the play teach us about parent-child relationships?

24. Who was your favourite character? Why did you enjoy this character?

25. Which character did you dislike most? Explain your view.

26. What are the main themes and issues in this play?

CLASSROOM QUESTIONS GUIDES

Short books of questions, designed to save teachers time and lead to rewarding classroom experiences.

www.SceneBySceneGuides.com

www.facebook.com/scenebyscene